ARIANA AFGHAN AIRLINES CO. LTD.

دآريانا افغان هوائي شركت

Passenger Ticket and Baggage Check
(For Domestic Carriage Only)

هر مسافر باید این تکت و مخصوصا شرایط
داخل صفحه را دقیقا مطالعه نماید. در حفاظت
تکت توجه نماید زیرا در مقابل تکتهای مفقود
شده اعاده" پول مجاز نیست. میعاد اعتبار تکت
یکسال بوده و بعدا قابل استفاده و ریفند نمیباشد.

Each passenger should carefully examine
this ticket, particularly the conditions inside.

Ensure safe custody of your ticket.
No refund is permissible against lost ticket.
Ticket validity is for one year. Expired ticket
is not good for transportation or refund.

Safi Airways TRANSFER

ECONOMY bmi boarding pass

name of passenger: MATTHEWS/JENNIFER

ETKT 236 960820202039

from FNA
to LHR

carrier BD flight no / class 968 date H 23AUG seat 0145

BMI

29D

Business Class Boarding Pass

Name:
Flight No
Date:
From:
To:
Seat No: 13 D
Tkt No:
Gate Board Time

BRITI... Kam Air Economy Class Boarding Pass

NAME OF P... MATTHE...
BA/BL...
FROM ENTR...
TO LOND...

FLIGHT N... BA
GATE GA...
PCS. CK...
1

Name:
Flight No
Date:
From:
To: 25 E
Sea... Board Time
Tkt No: Gate

MATTHEWS/JENNIFER

KQ 0576 18AUG12
FROM: NAIROBI/NBO

CLASS: M SEAT: 18C

5 G

BA 035422

Airline/Flight Date
Via

BA 035422

Airline/Flight Date
Via

JNB

BA 035
JNB

Carnaval da Victória de 1981
Carnaval dela Victoire — 1981
Carnival of Victory — 1981

June 7th 1987
Luanda
am waiting for a plane/helicopter
to travel north - and have
been for the last few days -
have only been arrested
once - haven't caught cholera
(there's meant to be an epidemic
and haven't taken many pix as
there's a complete paranoia about
photography. Hopefully things
will get better - if not will be

there are 2 copies of each - 1 to
go to her 1 to retain - her address
in my work address book under
'book-keeper' - her name is Ebie
if this is too complicated, forget it
hope you're both well - lots of love
Jenny x

LONDON

D0783597

CHILDREN
GROWING UP WITH
WAR

JENNY MATTHEWS

FRANKLIN WATTS
LONDON•SYDNEY

CONTENTS

Countries highlighted in **bold** have an explanation of how conflict has affected them on pages 46–47.

First published in 2014 by Franklin Watts
338 Euston Road, London NW1 3BH

Franklin Watts Australia, Level 17/207
Kent Street, Sydney NSW 2000

Text and photographs © Jenny Matthews 2014
Design © Franklin Watts 2014

All rights reserved.

Contributing author and editor: Ruth Thomson
Executive editor: Adrian Cole
Art direction: Peter Scoulding
Design: Jason Billin

A CIP catalogue record for this book
is available from the British Library.

Dewey Classification: 303.6'6'083

(hb) ISBN: 978 1 4451 2347 9
(Library ebook) ISBN: 978 1 4451 3226 6

Printed in China

Franklin Watts is a division of Hachette Children's
Books, an Hachette UK company.

www.hachette.co.uk

"FOR ALL THOSE CHILDREN WHOSE LIVES HAVE BEEN TOUCHED BY WAR, MAY THEIR FUTURES BE MARKED BY PEACE.
MAY THOSE WHO HAVE HAD HAPPY PEACEFUL CHILDHOODS, BE INSPIRED TO THINK ABOUT CHANGING THE WORLD.
TO THOSE OF YOU WHO WANT TO BE PHOTOGRAPHERS, POWER TO YOUR PICTURES." J.M.

NOTE TO PARENTS AND TEACHERS

Due to the nature of this book and the Internet, and the content of the websites featured on page 47, the Publisher strongly advises that young persons' Internet access is supervised by a responsible adult.

Haringey Libraries	
YY	
Askews & Holts	17-Mar-2014
303.6608	
	HAJR10/12/13

INTRODUCTION

WHY AM I A PHOTOGRAPHER?

I became a photographer more than 30 years ago because I wanted to change the world. Since then I have travelled to many conflict zones to take photographs, but I've found that, unfortunately, taking pictures rarely changes anything. However, it has given me a way to communicate. I can tell people's stories, and hope that my photos will encourage others to get involved – whether by giving money, voting, lobbying politicians or becoming a voice against injustice.

The main focus of my work is to document what goes on behind the action of front-line war. I'm interested in how it affects women, children and families in their day-to-day lives.

CHILDREN AND WAR

How would you feel if you lost your home and had to flee from your own country? Imagine losing some, or all, of your family either as a direct result of fighting, or indirectly through illness and disease. You might have to work to support your family or fight and kill other people just to survive. And how can you go to school if it's being used as an army command outpost, and all the books have been destroyed?

This is the reality for too many children and their families in the world. Today, children are growing up with war – the consequences of which they'll live with for the rest of their lives.

This book features just some of the thousands of photographs I've taken. They've been organised into six chapters, each one showing ways in which children are affected by war. These children don't make war, but are dragged into it – usually by adults, and usually by men. These chapters can be linked back to the UN Convention on the Rights of the Child – see page 5.

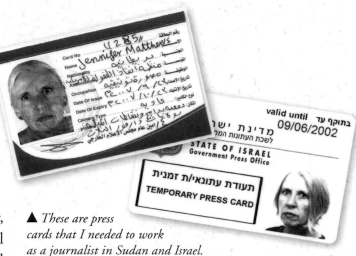

▲ *These are press cards that I needed to work as a journalist in Sudan and Israel.*

WORKING FREELANCE

I'm a freelance photojournalist, which means I don't work for a particular company or organisation. Sometimes, I accompany a journalist on a story for a magazine or newspaper. At other times, I'm commissioned by non-government organisations (NGO), such as ActionAid or CARE International, that provide emergency help. They need photographs to inform the public, as well as raise money. Other times, I travel to places to work on a major project of my own, looking at women and war.

◀ *Many countries I travel to require visas. These pages from my passport show the visas I had for **Uganda** and Chad.*

▶ *This hamsa, or hand of Fatima (hand of Miriam in Judaism), was a present from **Iraq**. I like to think it protects me on my assignments.*

3

GETTING INTO A CONFLICT ZONE

Often, the biggest challenge for a journalist is the logistics of getting to a trouble spot and working safely once there. Research is essential. I use the library and Internet for background information and watch news reports, talk to experts, and learn a bit of the language.

Local people are invaluable. Sometimes I pay a "fixer"—a local person with good contacts—to help me find people and places and to translate. At other times, I work with local organizations. I try to travel as discreetly as possible, but in some dangerous situations photographers team up for safety and support and to share travel expenses.

▲ *Unlike me, Farida, who I worked with in* **Afghanistan***, knew that the red-and-white stones meant the road had just been demined, and was safe to walk along.*

This is my essential camera equipment. I try to travel as lightly as possible, taking only carry-on luggage if it's a short trip. The less you carry, the faster you can move (especially getting on and off planes!).

Card reader

Memory cards

Portable hard drive for storing and backing up downloaded pictures

USB hard drive that can be taken to a shop to get prints made

60 mm macro lens

Flash

18–200 mm lens

Laptop computer for downloading photos on memory cards

12–24 mm wide-angle lens

Spare batteries

Lens cleaner

Digital SLR camera

▲ *On every trip, I carry a notebook for keeping a record of places, people, and their comments. If I have time, I write a diary.*

▶ *Money from some of the places I have visited. It's important to have local currency—you can't pay by debit card in most places.*

4

It was very emotional to realise what Phuong had been denied – the very sense that I rely on for my work.

The UN Convention on the Rights of the Child is an agreement that gives everyone under the age of 18 key rights designed to help protect them. Unfortunately, war can mean that these rights are forgotten, leaving children vulnerable to abuse and violence.

- The right to enjoy these rights, regardless of race, colour, sex, religion, national or social origin
- The right to develop individual abilities
- The right to a name and nationality
- The right to adequate nutrition and medical care
- The right to special care if disabled
- The right to affection, love and understanding
- The right to free education, to learn to be a useful member of society, and to full opportunity for play and recreation
- The right to be among the first to receive relief in times of disaster
- The right to protection against all forms of neglect, cruelty and exploitation
- The right to be brought up in a spirit of peace

How many of these rights do you think would be affected by war?

FINDING PHUONG

The effects of war were brought home to me when I was photographing in Vietnam long after the war was over. In the 1960s, the situation in this country had shaped my politics and made me aware of the part that film and photography play in recording history. When I visited an orphanage in Saigon, one little girl named Phuong was wearing sunglasses. When she took them off, I was shocked to see that she had no eyes.

It is presumed that her mother was poisoned by Agent Orange, a chemical sprayed over forests during the Vietnam War by US planes, 30 years earlier. The chemical has remained in the ecosystem, and is still continuing to cause birth defects.

"Although I may shoot a photograph in 125th of a second – so all the photos in this book add up to less than a minute – I spent hours travelling, chatting and listening before I took them."

▲ *These boys have made their own toy guns from wood and other scrap materials.*

HOME AND DISPLACEMENT

When there's a war going on some people have no choice but to stay in their house or apartment, and hope they are not bombed or attacked. If possible, families flee, perhaps to safety within their country, and become known as Internally Displaced People (IDPs). They might end up constructing temporary homes, sleeping in a school, camping in a park or renting rooms in another town.

If people cross an international border, they become refugees. If they are lucky, the international community provides help – although appeals rarely raise enough funds. Fleeing war puts great strain on family finances. People sell jewellery and other valuables just to survive.

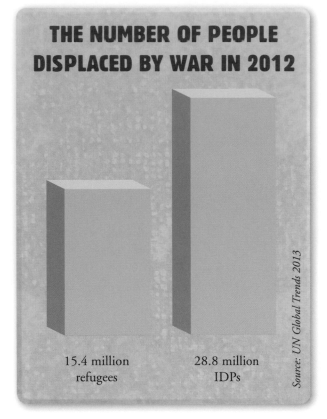

THE NUMBER OF PEOPLE DISPLACED BY WAR IN 2012

15.4 million refugees

28.8 million IDPs

Source: UN Global Trends 2013

*In the **Democratic Republic of the Congo (DRC)**, displaced people constructed temporary homes out of branches and plastic sheeting.*

KIBATI CAMP FOR THE DISPLACED, GOMA, DRC. NOVEMBER, 2008

I went to Goma in the Democratic Republic of the Congo (DRC) to report on the humanitarian crisis facing people there. Communities had fled rebels, who were terrorising them, and ended up in camps. Here, people had to build improvised shelters for themselves on hard, uncomfortable volcanic rock. As I walked around, I spotted Fraha, resplendent in an orange dress and scarf, sitting next to her hut with her baby son, Shukuru. I am always impressed by how women in the most difficult conditions manage to take pride in their appearance. They are neat and clean, in spite of having no electricity or running water. A nearby family asked me to photograph them in front of their new home.

▲ *Fraha and her baby, Shukuru, at Kibati Camp.*

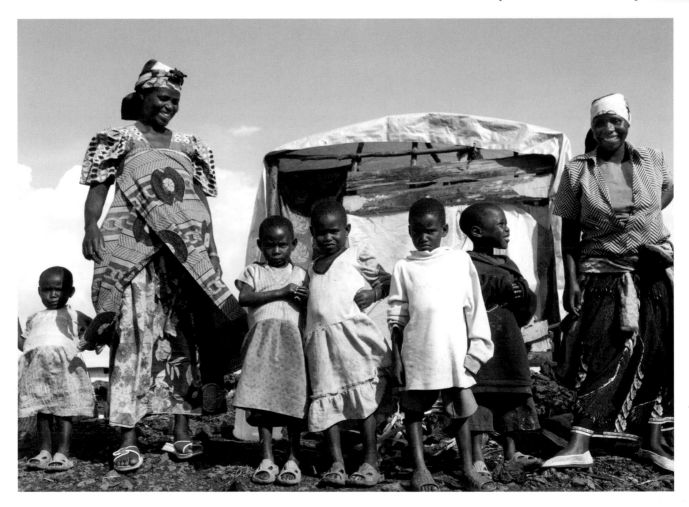

▲ *Nyirrahabimana (second from left) is proud of the shelter that she and her sister Maombi (right) built from bits of scrap wood and old plastic food sacks.*

DEKWANEH, BEIRUT, LEBANON. AUGUST, 2006

When pieces of paper came fluttering down onto her apartment block, Lina knew instantly what they meant. On each one was a message from the Israeli army telling people to leave the area of Dahiyeh, a poor district of Beirut, before a bombing raid began.

Lina grabbed her two daughters, three-year-old Aya and four-month-old Maia, and stuffed some clothes into a plastic bag. She left a message for her husband who was at work, and fled to a school in nearby Dekwaneh. Throughout Beirut and the southern towns of Tyre and Sidon, hundreds of schools offered shelter to people like Lina, who had suddenly become homeless.

Lina, Aya and Maia camp in a classroom, thankful to have a roof over their heads, but uncertain of when they'll be able to return home.

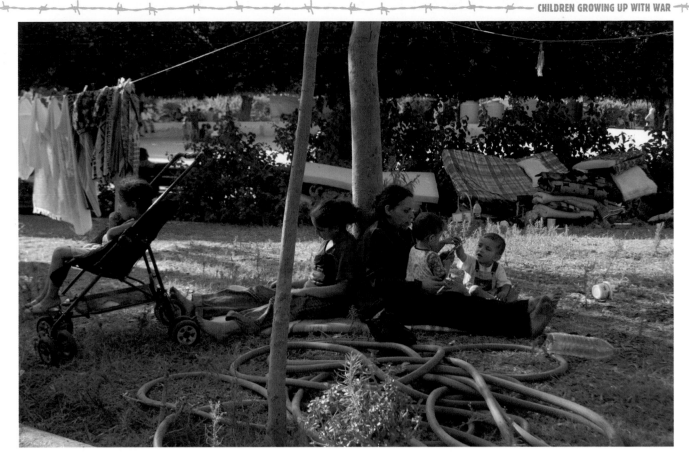

▲ The hoses used for watering the plants in the park came in handy for washing clothes and keeping cool in the boiling summer heat.

SANAYEH, BEIRUT, LEBANON. AUGUST, 2006

Hundreds of other families, including Azzat and her eight children, were forced to camp on the grass in a local park. In the middle of the night the bomber planes flew over. The explosions as bombs landed and destroyed buildings were terrifying.

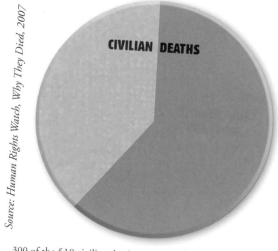

Source: Human Rights Watch, Why They Died, 2007

CIVILIAN DEATHS

300 of the 510 civilian deaths in **Lebanon** during the 34-day conflict with Israel were women and children.

▲ I was standing next to Azzat on a Sunday afternoon when a bomb dropped nearby. She grabbed a child and froze in complete panic.

9

RAMADA REFUGEE CAMP, TUNISIA. MAY, 2011

In the rush to flee **Libya** for the safety of a refugee camp just over the border in Tunisia, Mona forgot her spot cream. It's the one thing she wishes she'd grabbed. Now she's living in a tent, sleeping on a mat on the sand, with just the clothes she was wearing when they fled in the night. And her skin isn't getting better. Of course, she also has more serious things to think about.

"We've left behind our family, our homes, our goods. It's not a life here – in Nalut we had a lovely home. Here we can only read the Qur'an, tidy up and organise play activities for the younger children. Because we fled in fear, we left everything behind, so we only have the clothes we are wearing. We've been praying for our families in Nalut. We've been very worried. This morning, before sunrise, we felt the vibrations from the mortars. I prayed for my home, my street, I prayed for hope, for my goals. My brother is fighting with a group of friends. They all look out for each other.

▲ *Nineteen-year-old Mona, outside her tent. She wanted to hide her identity to protect her family, who are still in Libya.*

It's been over a month since I saw him, but my father goes back when the fighting dies down and says he's in good health and really keen to carry on fighting."

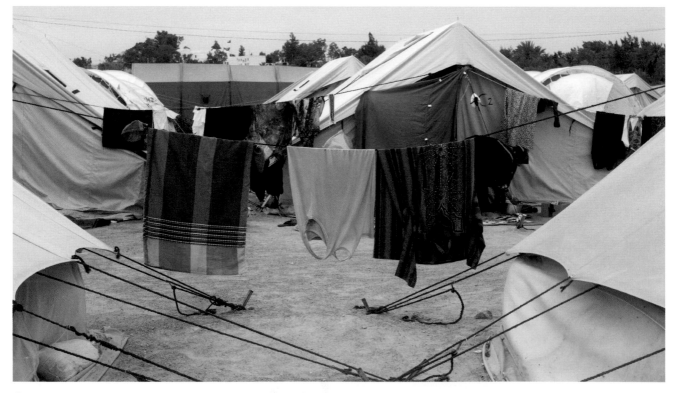

▲ *More than 1,500 people spent several months living in these overcrowded tents in Ramada.*

AMMAN, JORDAN. APRIL, 2013

Although many refugees seek safety in camps in a neighbouring country, many others make their own way to towns and cities there. Here, they find shelter with family members or rent rooms, and try to find work. If a conflict goes on for a long time, as in the case of **Syria**, this can put a strain on families and their finances.

When I asked some Syrian refugees in Jordan what they had brought with them when they fled from their homes, everyone said just a small bag of clothes. One family had a room to sleep 18 people. Each night they unfurled neatly folded blankets to make the floor a bit more comfortable.

▲ *This family could only afford to rent a single room. There is no fridge, no washing machine, no cooker – there isn't even a bathroom. Everyone shares a single toilet and a sink for washing.*

◀ *Hassan, aged 15, explained to me that he brought only the clothes he was wearing and a pair of shoes.*

▲ *This is the shared sink in the small room in Jordan.*

11

THE PHOTOGRAPHER'S PERSPECTIVE

I'm aware that, as a photographer, I "parachute" into people's lives and spend a short amount of time talking, listening and photographing. Then I leave them, to go back to a world with electricity, running water, a choice of what to eat and the freedom to travel. I think it's easy to forget how lucky we are. When I'm taking photographs I have to focus on the reason I'm there – to report back, to get my photos published and to share information and stories with the rest of the world.

In 2007, I travelled to Goz Bagar camp in Chad for CARE. I was there to photograph the work they were doing with Sudanese refugees who had fled from the conflict in **Darfur**. They use my photographs to illustrate stories and articles on their website and in their promotional material.

While I was at Goz Bagar camp, I met a mother and her family. She had left everything behind, and I recorded what she said to me in one of my notebooks:

Mariam Issak Adam, aged 30, with her four children – Ousman Issak, aged 10; Nadjoi Issak, aged 7; Mahama Issak, aged 5 and Yakhoub Issak, aged 3 – at Goz Bagar camp.

"The war sent us from our village. Before we had breakfast, armed men came to our village. They killed nine people, including my husband, and so we decided to leave because of the lack of security. Life is difficult now. I've lost my husband and I've my children to look after. I've no hope of going back. The men who attacked us are still there, next to the village. I brought nothing with us, no money, no goods, nothing."

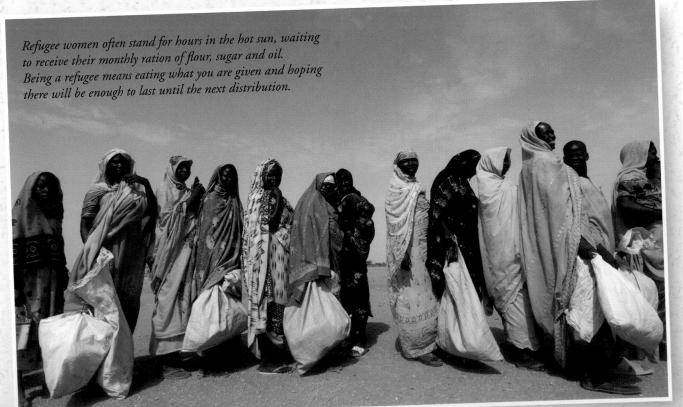

Refugee women often stand for hours in the hot sun, waiting to receive their monthly ration of flour, sugar and oil. Being a refugee means eating what you are given and hoping there will be enough to last until the next distribution.

LIFE FOR REFUGEES

The difference between my life and that of refugees is enormous. I am always very humbled that people who have lost virtually everything can be bothered to talk to me about their lives, and insist on sharing what little they have – always offering me food and tea.

In Qawala camp, near Sulaimaniya, Kurdistan, in 2008, I met 3-year-old Taybeh and her mother. They fled from the sectarian violence between Sunni and Shi'ites in northern Iraq. The camp was home to around 3,000 people, just some of the 2.5 million Iraqis homeless in their own country.

▲ *Taybeh and her mother live on a landfill site in a structure made from an old tent and plastic sheeting. I think they were laughing at me taking a photo of the washing up. At home they'd had a proper kitchen, with running water and a washing machine.*

PERMANENT CAMPS

Sometimes people spend a few months in tents. Others, like the Palestinians in Gaza and the West Bank, build houses where their tents were but still refer to their communities as "camps", even though they've lived there for more than 60 years.

I met Tahane in Netzarim, Gaza, in 2009 after the Israeli Defense Forces launched Operation Cast Lead. She told me how loudspeakers had told her to leave her house. She had just enough time to pack a few things and scoop up her three young children before the air strike. Her house was completely destroyed.

Tahane stands with her children in front of her home. She's come back to see what she can salvage from the ruins.

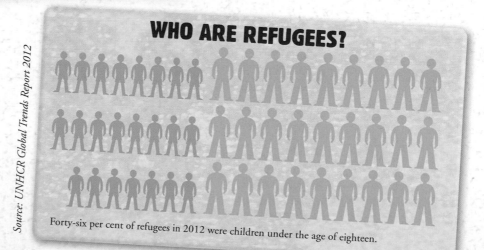

Source: UNHCR Global Trends Report 2012

WHO ARE REFUGEES?

Forty-six per cent of refugees in 2012 were children under the age of eighteen.

FAMILY

War breaks families apart through anxiety, separation and death. Traditionally in war, it is fathers who are killed during fighting. This can be devastating for children, and life for the family becomes much harder, especially if he was the only one earning money.

However, different types of conflict mean that children are being caught up in war in other ways, such as when missiles miss their targets (as happened to Nabeela's family, see right). In some cases, young people are sent away for safety, and grow up without their parents. Others are kidnapped and forced to become soldiers. Entire families can become casualties of war.

▲ *Nabeela holds a photo of her 12-year-old son Mohammed, killed by a bomb that injured her other two sons. One lost an eye and the other lost both legs.*

▲ *Ali with a photograph of his son, who disappeared on his way to Australia. Ali thinks he might have been amongst a group of asylum seekers whose boat sank.*

MEDENINE TRANSIT CENTRE FOR LIBYAN REFUGEES, TUNISIA. MAY, 2011

Afaf is the mother of six children. Her husband was killed in Libya fighting Colonel Muammar Gaddafi's regime. Having fled to Tunisia for safety, she now faces change in her country as head of the family.

"We come from the city of Nalut, up on the mountain. We ran away because of the shelling. We are not running away because we are afraid of death, but because we women fear being attacked. The men brought the women here and went back to fight. My husband, Abdul Hameed, was killed in Nalut. He taught mechanics and had experience of guns because he did his national service. He was an instructor to other rebels. We want Libya to change. First, we want decent education. The children's life is zero. We want a good economy and a good health system. I want a good future for my children."

▲ *Afaf holds up a photograph of her husband who was killed in Libya.*

AFGHANISTAN

In many places, decades of war have created a culture of violence and reliance on the father to provide everything for the family. People are killed over petty arguments and children are used to solve family problems.

In Afghanistan there is a tradition called "baad", whereby a girl is given away to solve a dispute. In 2009, I met Hulya – a 14-year-old girl. Her father had killed his brother in a fight over some wood. To stop the two families fighting, Hulya is now married to her 15-year-old cousin, Humdillah.

Young girls are also used to rescue families from the poverty that comes with conflict. Perhaps the father has been killed or injured, and is unable to work and earn money. When a marriage is arranged, the bride's family receives a dowry, and this money can make a big difference to them. For widows, though, it is hard to negotiate a good bride price and ensure their daughters are treated well. Women can be mistreated by their husbands, and some run away.

▲ *Neither Humdillah nor Hulya wants to be married, but they also know they have no choice.*

Angiza (not her real name) ran away from an uncle who was trying to sell her in Kabul. Fortunately, she was able to find a safe shelter, very unusual in a country with no social services. Women are often put in prison for running away.

▲ *Sahat Gul has arranged the marriage of her daughter, 10-year-old Gul, to a middle-aged man.*

▲ *Sefura with two of her daughters and one of her sons. Her youngest daughter holds a photo of her father.*

When I met Sefura in Kabul, Afghanistan, she was saddened, both by the loss of her husband and by the effect this had on her daughters' lives.

"The Taliban killed my husband in 2001. He was in the military. I have four daughters and two sons. The sons work pushing carts and selling vegetables.

Five months after I was widowed, my sixteen-year-old daughter disappeared. She had been engaged since she was three months old. I don't know what happened to her. Her fiancé's family was furious. They demanded two daughters in her place and forced two of my daughters to marry. There was nothing I could do. If my husband had not died, we could have looked after our first daughter better, so she would not have disappeared. He could have protected us. It is because I am a widow that all these things have happened."

War, and the subsequent loss of family members, makes children grow up too quickly. They lose their childhood and take on adult roles. This is most dramatic in the case of child abductees. Many recent wars in Africa, in particular in **Sierra Leone**, Liberia, Uganda and the DRC, have seen the brutalisation of children, who are often drugged, and then forced to kill. Child soldiers sometimes spend years in "small boy units", where they adapt to their environment and the power they get from using weapons. It is very difficult to reintegrate these children back into their communities afterwards.

▲ *Clutching a Kalashnikov gun, this young boy is guarding a restaurant in Freetown, the capital of Sierra Leone.*

CASE STUDY: PEACE CLUB, BARLONYO. UGANDA, 2011

Susan, a young mother, is part of a peace club in Barlonyo. It's a group of former child abductees, who support each other and re-enact the massacre carried out by the Lord's Resistance Army (LRA). It helps them to explain to the community what happened, and why there has to be reconciliation.

Susan is dressed up as Joseph Kony (below), the leader of the LRA. Kony is responsible for abducting thousands of children in northern Uganda and turning them into child soldiers, who then terrorised and killed villagers.

Susan is very familiar with the LRA. They abducted her and forced her to kill a baby. Although only a child herself, she had to become the "wife" of a LRA soldier. When the Ugandan army rescued her, she was pregnant. She now has a 7-year-old son.

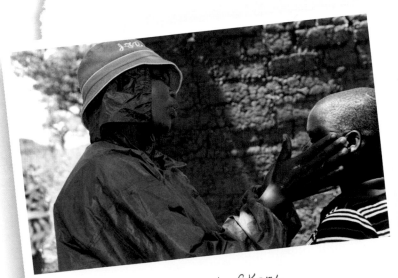

Susan acts the part of Kony.

Barlonyo, Susan's community, was the scene of a massacre in 2004. The LRA commander launched an operation called "Kill Every Living Thing" at a camp for displaced villagers. There were lots of young people in the camp, and the LRA wanted to abduct them and force them to become part of their group.

That afternoon, more than 300 people were killed and hundreds of young people taken away. People were burned inside their straw huts and hacked to death with machetes.

After years living in the bush with the LRA, it was very hard for child abductees to return to their communities once the war ended. They felt guilty and many villagers blamed them for killing their family members.

Boys act the part of abducted child soldiers.

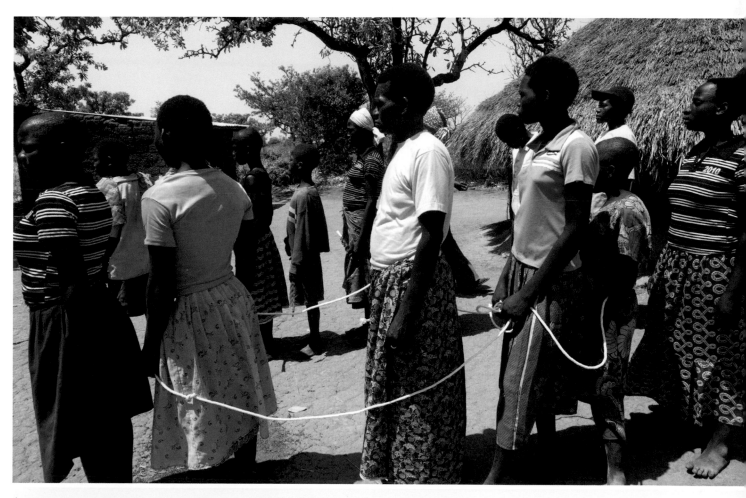

▲ Young people, playing the part of villagers, are roped together and taken away to be shot.

19

THE PHOTOGRAPHER'S PERSPECTIVE

▲ *Samah, her husband, Darwish, and their four children fled from Syria to Jordan in April, 2013.*

People often ask me how I can bear to work in difficult situations. I think it helps if you know why you are taking pictures. Some people think a journalist should be a neutral, uninvolved observer, to just write or photograph. For me, I want to be as close as possible to my subject, to try to understand what people are going through. This usually means taking sides. It also means spending time with people – which they really value – and taking time to listen and observe.

As a photographer I want to portray intimate situations, but at the same time the camera distances me – there is a lens between me and reality. Sometimes this means it is possible to photograph something quite horrible, and save the emotional reaction to it for later.

▶ *Fatem and her teddy. Fatem's mother said, "The area was being attacked, so we hid in a shelter. As I left the house, my two-year-old daughter grabbed her teddy. She held on as tightly to the teddy as she did to me, so we couldn't leave it behind. Her father gave it to her on her first birthday."*

I think this way of making sense of each situation enabled me to work in **Rwanda**, when I travelled there during the genocide in 1994.

GENOCIDE IN RWANDA, 1994

In 1994, more than 800,000 people were killed during the 100 days of genocide in Rwanda. Every family has a story of loss and pain – some lost 20 relatives, some 30. They were all killed in the most savage way. At the time, Rwanda seemed to be a country of widows and orphans.

The people who did the killing, and others who were part of their community and saw what happened, fled over the border to neighbouring Zaire (now the DRC). Lots of children were separated from their families on the long walk to the border. It is thought some families deliberately 'lost' their small children, either knowing they could move faster without them, or hoping they would be taken care of by a foreign aid agency, and therefore have a better future.

▲ *I came across 5-year-old Kamonzi in hospital, one of the thousands of orphans traumatised by what he had seen and unable to speak.*

Sometimes I do stop taking photos and help. No picture is worth someone dying for. Life is always more important than photography.

▲ *When you see an abandoned child, your instinct is to help – to take them somewhere safe. In an emergency situation there might not be many options. During a cholera epidemic in Zaire, the only possibility for this child was one of the tents that some aid workers set up as an orphanage.*

21

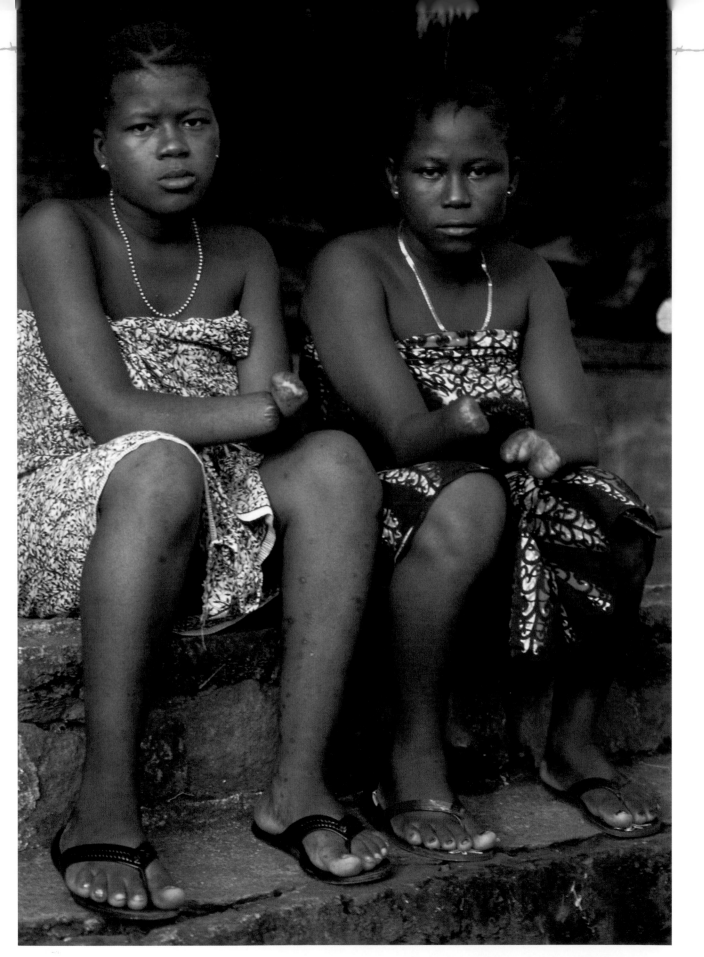

▲ *In Sierra Leone, rebels (young boys, often high on drugs) terrorised and mutilated people with knives – cutting off their hands. Mariatu, aged 15 (left) and Adamasay, aged 14 (right) survived, but many others bled to death, because there were no doctors or nurses with equipment to save them. Mariatu is now a UNICEF Special Representative for Children and Armed Conflict.*

HEALTH

In the course of war, bodies and minds are damaged and destroyed. Besides deaths from bombings and guns, many people die because of poor health facilities – hospitals, clinics and even ambulances may be destroyed. It might even be too dangerous to take people to get treatment.

People's health is also affected by the poverty that war brings. Adults lose their jobs and therefore their income. As a result people, especially children, die from hunger, from lack of access to medical facilities or even clean water.

▲ *Parents, whose babies died of hunger, pray with members of the community at their graves in the Syakamak village cemetery in Afghanistan.*

In the camps set up in Zaire after the Rwanda genocide, there was a massive cholera epidemic caused by the lack of toilets and clean water.

Women often give birth prematurely in conflict situations, because of stress and anxiety, and then have to care for a newborn baby in dirty conditions. I've seen babies die because their mothers had no milk to feed them. Young children have no choice but to drink dirty water. They get sick and then quickly become dehydrated. Normally, this could be easily treated with a solution of salt and sugar – but this works only if the water is clean. Health programmes become disrupted in wartime, too. Without vaccination, children become vulnerable to diseases, such as measles, that they would normally be immunised against.

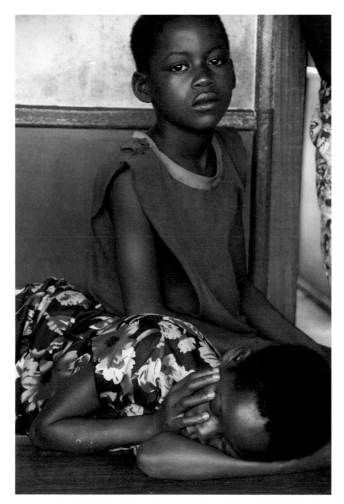

◄ *A young refugee from the DRC with malaria waits to see a nurse in a village clinic. Sleeping under an insecticide-treated net greatly reduces the chances of getting malaria, which is a killer disease if not treated. During conflict, people do not prioritise the use of nets.*

▼ *Invented by two French doctors, Plumpy'Nut is a soft peanut-based paste. It is high in calories and rich in protein, so children with acute malnutrition can gain weight very quickly.*

War brings other hidden health hazards, too. Dangerous chemicals, such as depleted uranium used in shells fired in Iraq, can remain in the ecosystem and affect people's health years later. Children collect the scrap metal to sell, and play in the burned-out military vehicles – which can be highly radioactive. This poisons their bodies and can lead to cancer or birth defects when they have their own children.

▲ *A girl in Basra, Iraq, walks past a troop carrier, which still measured considerable radiation a year after being hit by a depleted-uranium-tipped rocket.*

Some weapons, such as small land mines, are designed to kill and injure soldiers. But these are left in the ground long after any war has ended. When children in Afghanistan picked up what they thought were plastic butterflies, they ended up being badly injured. Even after years of painstaking work clearing and defusing land mines, many still remain hidden.

◄ *In some countries, more than 30 per cent of land mine casualties are under the age of 15. Shabnam, an Afghan, is one of them.*

LAND MINES

There are thought to be somewhere in the region of 100 million active land mines and explosive devices in the world. In 2011 there were 4,286 reported casualties, of which 42 per cent were children.

A growing child's artificial limb needs replacing every six months. A ten-year-old mine amputee, with a life expectancy of another 50 years, will need 25 artificial limbs over his or her lifetime.

Sources: International Campaign to Ban Landmines and One World/CARE

CASE STUDY: MENTAL HEALTH, BAOBAB CENTRE. LONDON, 2013

Besides physical disabilities, the stress and fear of living with war can cause children to have nightmares, to lose their confidence and suffer long term damage to their sense of security and comfort.

The Baobab Centre for Young Survivors in Exile works with young asylum seekers who have arrived unaccompanied in the UK. Many of them have witnessed conflict and some have been forced to perpetrate violence. The centre provides therapy and practical support to help them deal with the long-lasting trauma.

When I asked students at a centre for young war survivors in London to hold something that expressed their hope for the future, these were some of their choices:

▲ *Night after night of heavy bombing terrified everyone. This drawing shows one child's view of the violence that occurred during nights of heavy bombing in Lebanon.*

SCISSORS
"I want to be a high-fashion hairdresser. That's my future."

A JUG OF WATER
"The water is clean and clear – so I hope my future will be fine and good, not like the problems I had back home. This water represents a good future when everything will be fine."

EMPTY HANDS
"The future is blurry. Anything could happen. There's no certainty to it."

BOOK AND PEN
"My dream is to continue my education."

GUITAR AND BALLS
"Music is inspiration. Football and basketball are the whole world."

MONEY
"Money is life. No money, no life. Money is food. If you don't have money, you can't buy your travel card, you can't buy clothes, you can't eat."

FOLDER OF COLLEGE WORK
"Education is the key. I love geography, because it gives an understanding of how the world today is evolving."

THE PHOTOGRAPHER'S PERSPECTIVE

I think many of us take health care for granted. If we need a doctor, dentist or optician, we just make an appointment. In a conflict zone, getting medical help is not so easy. As a journalist, it is important that I stay healthy, so I don't become a burden on others. I carry a basic first-aid kit containing things such as aspirins and plasters.

▲ *Girls clean latrines in the DRC. Several of the doors are missing, giving users no privacy. Thirty per cent of refugee camps do not have adequate latrines. Sharing a latrine with three or more families greatly increases the risk of cholera.*

Refugees in camps can often get access to these things too, but other essentials can be harder to find. Mosquitoes spread the disease malaria, so it is important to sleep under a mosquito net. Quite often there aren't enough of these for everybody who needs one, especially children and pregnant women. Cholera is another terrible disease. In camps, this can be spread by poor hygiene and dirty drinking water. I'm very careful to drink clean water, but the toilets can be a problem – it's best not to be squeamish and a long skirt can be very useful!

At the Za'atri camp in Jordan for Syrian refugees, Qamar collects water for her family. The United Nations Refugee Agency (UNHCR) estimates that more than half of all refugee camps cannot provide the recommended daily minimum of 20 litres of water per person per day.

UNHCR
The UN

CASE STUDY: TRAINING MIDWIVES. AFGHANISTAN, 2011

One of the most memorable trips I've been on was with Merlin – the medical NGO (see page 47) – to visit a training school for midwives in Afghanistan. Young village teenage girls spend 18 months training and then return to work in their villages, where they are often the only health worker. Much of Afghanistan is very difficult to access, because of high mountains and bad winter weather. Road blocks, fear of kidnapping and lack of transport mean women are unlikely to go to a hospital to give birth, so these midwives are essential.

I spent a week in town with the young women, but it was considered too dangerous for me to go with a midwife to a village to see her in action. A western photographer could have jeopardised her work and provoked the local Taliban into attacking. For me, it was more important for them to continue working safely – although it was disappointing not to follow my story to its end.

▲ *Learning to check a newborn baby's breathing.*

▲ *Girls learn to administer injections by practising on satsumas.*

This newly-trained midwife is about to set off to her village.

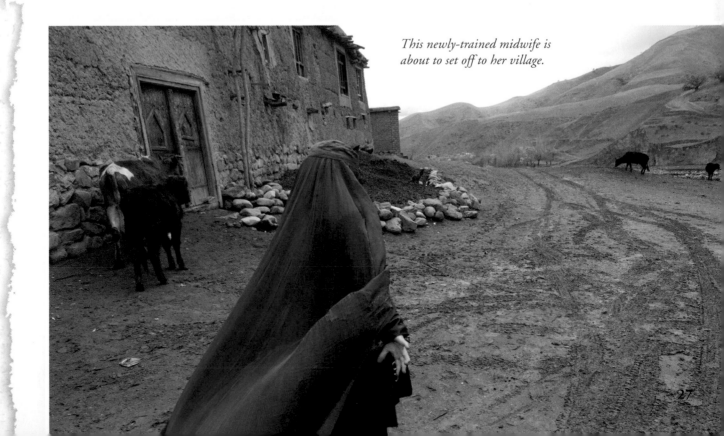

27

WORK

Parents always hope that their children will have a better life than their own. They want them to have a good education and a safe upbringing. But the reality is that many families survive only because of the help their children provide – by doing unpaid jobs such as farm work, collecting water and firewood, and looking after siblings or the family's animals.

War makes the situation worse when the family income is reduced. This can happen if a parent is away fighting or loses their job as a result of the upheavals brought by conflict. Electricity may be cut off, so workplaces close. Children can end up begging or helping someone out in return for food.

▲ *In refugee camps, like this one in Central African Republic (CAR), girls don't have to walk as far to get water as they would in their villages. However, they are still likely to miss school, as they wait their turn in the long queue at the camp water tap.*

▼ *In Afghanistan, most people have no gas or electricity and depend on firewood for heating and cooking. As the area around the city becomes deforested, boys cycle into the countryside to collect whatever they can find, either for their family or to sell.*

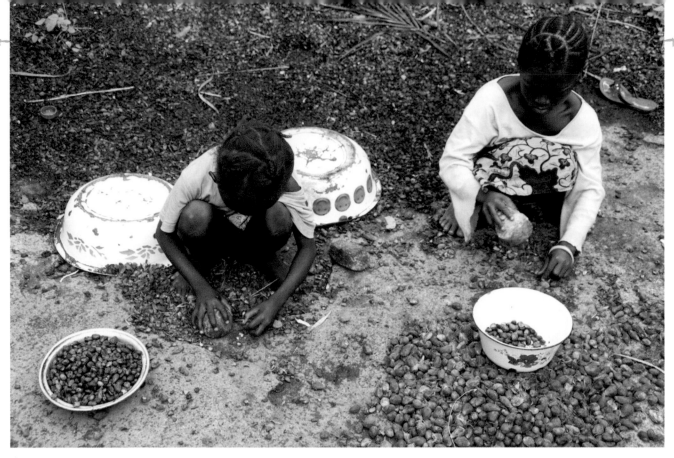

▲ *These children in Sierra Leone crack open palm oil nuts, which can be processed for their rich oil. The children are contributing to the family income by doing this repetitive job, leaving their parents free to farm their land to grow food for their family. After fighting stopped, fields were overgrown and needed a lot of work to return them to productive use.*

▲ *Maryam and her granddaughter collect small sticks to use as kindling from their wheat field in the Herat province of Afghanistan.*

AFGHANISTAN

The poverty that accompanies war means children often become breadwinners for their families. This is especially the case in Afghanistan. The large number of widows means the children, particularly boys, have the responsibility of earning some cash – perhaps by carrying goods in the market or minding animals. Girls, like Majan, often weave, as this painstaking work, which needs small nimble fingers, can be done in the home.

> When I was 16, I got married. I'd already lost my father and brothers during the war. After one year of marriage, my husband was killed in fighting so I came back to my mother's house. To earn some money to help my mother, I went to another house to weave, but now I'm much happier because I have a loom at home and I can weave at home and then sell the carpets – I make 5-metre long ones which sell for $60.

In Kabul, Afghanistan's capital, I've seen little gangs of children carrying sacks as big as themselves. Sometimes they collect waste paper and plastic to sell to recyclers, or twigs from the park to use as kindling. Children also go to bread shops to collect stale naan bread. This traditional bread goes hard very quickly. What isn't sold within a few hours is often given to the poor. Bread with weak tea is the basic meal for thousands of people in poverty, especially for those who have fled to the cities for safety from the fighting, and have no land on which to grow food.

▶ *In desperate times, people take desperate measures. In a market place in Kurdistan, I saw this tiny girl, an Iraqi refugee from the south, selling chewing gum, rather unwillingly. Her mother had sent her out, thinking people would feel sorry for her and buy something.*

WORKING CHILDREN

Almost 25 per cent of Afghan children aged 7–14 work.

Source: UNICEF 2009 Facts on child protection in Afghanistan.

▼ *Majan, aged 19, is a skilled carpet weaver.*

30

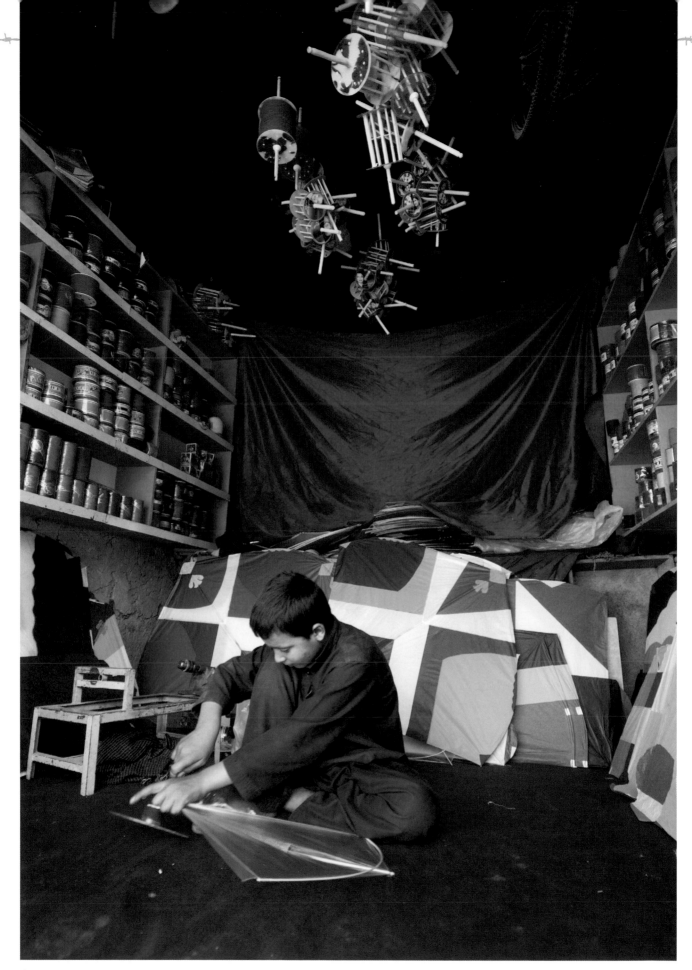

▲ *When the Taliban came to power in 1996, they banned kite flying, amongst other things. Now, 10-year-old Jamil is able to help in his father's workshop in Kabul. On Fridays (Afghanistan's day of rest) boys have kite-flying competitions.*

THE PHOTOGRAPHER'S PERSPECTIVE

Watching children weaving, I am overwhelmed that, even though they have never been to school and can't read or write, they can interpret a pattern on paper into a carpet. On the street, child vendors can calculate change without ever having been to a maths class.

A young boy minding sheep or goats is responsible for the animals in his care. He has to cope with being by himself all day and to make sure no animal is lost, injured or stolen, as he could never afford to replace it.

While I'm impressed by the skills working children like Hasmatullah have, I'm depressed by their lost childhood. They have almost no time for play.

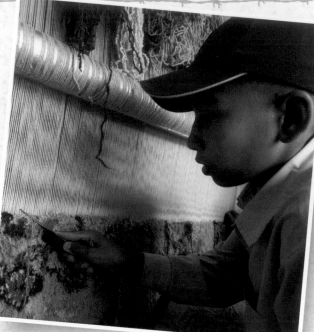

▲ *Hasmatullah Neami, aged 14. There are ten in his family – two parents, one grandmother, three brothers and three sisters.*

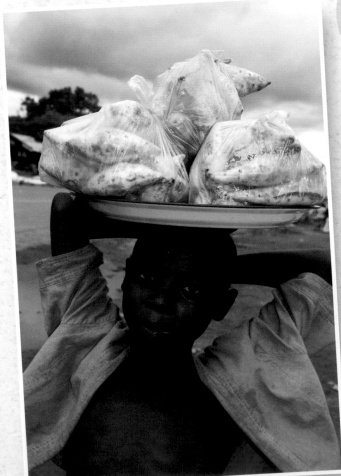

"I am the only one earning money in my family. My father was disabled in the war – a land mine exploded and he lost his hand. We were refugees in Iran and six years ago we returned to Kabul, When we could no longer pay the rent, we moved out of the city. Afghan children were not allowed to go to school in Iran, so I do not know how to read or write. I have been training to weave for six months and earning an income for my family. I earn $3 a day and when I finish the training, I hope I will find work as a trainee carpet weaver in Kabul."

◀ *Ibrahim sells sweet potatoes by the roadside in Sierra Leone.*

▲ *In the centre of Kabul, Afghanistan, it's hard to find anywhere for animals to graze, other than amongst the rubbish piled by the road. Looking after animals here means coping with traffic, too.*

CASE STUDY: PHOTOVOICE PROJECT. PAKISTAN, 2010

In Pakistan, many families have fled the danger of the northern states – brought by the war in Afghanistan – for big cities further south. In areas such as Rawalpindi, thousands of children end up working in order for their families to survive. I spent a couple of weeks on a Photovoice project, teaching photography to working children, who produced an exhibition about their lives.

▲ Girls Scavenging *by Sitara, who wrote, "These children are collecting rubbish, but they should be going to school."*

▲ Boy in a Workshop *by Hikmat, who wrote, "This is Ibrahim, he's 12. He used to come and study at this centre but then his parents insisted he went out to work."*

SCHOOL AND PLAY

For some children, the violence that war brings completely disrupts their education, destroying or closing schools. For those who make it into a camp though, classes are usually organised by international agencies such as UNICEF, Save the Children or Islamic Relief. These classes help provide some structure for children traumatised by the loss of their home and familiar surroundings. For some children this is their first experience of school.

▲ *In 2007, when I visited schools in camps for IDPs in Darfur, no-one moaned about doing gym in the boiling hot desert.*

Usually, the teachers are volunteers from the camp itself, and they understand the problems of concentration and distress that the pupils may face. The classes are often overcrowded, but the students appreciate having something to do.

KURDISTAN, 2008

In Kurdistan, the Iraqi children I met in their muddy camp were enrolled in local schools. This had many plus points – they met local children, they had trained teachers and they had a school with reasonable facilities.

But there were also negative points. Children struggled with the language, as everything was in Kurdish rather than Arabic, the language of southern Iraq. They were also embarrassed about where they lived, surrounded by mud, and it was difficult for them to keep their uniforms clean.

◄ *This little girl had put plastic bags over her shoes, so that they wouldn't be too muddy by the time she reached school.*

▲ *Grace was abducted from her school and forced to walk to Sudan. The experience of having to be the "wife" of a boy soldier has traumatised her, and made it hard for her to return to her village. Everyone knows what happened to her, but she has nowhere else to go.*

UGANDA, 2007

In northern Uganda, the LRA specifically abducted large numbers of boarding-school students – nearly all secondary schools have boarders (children who stay at school overnight) – because the distances between the school and their homes are too great. The abducted children became LRA fighters, "wives", cooks and porters.

GAZA, 2009

I went to Gaza just after the Israeli-named Operation Cast Lead. The three weeks of war resulted in more than 1,000 Palestinian and 13 Israeli deaths (four from "friendly fire"). A number of schools were destroyed by the bombing, but children returned to classes as soon as there was a ceasefire. Many had to study in temporary classrooms whilst theirs were being repaired.

▼ *Many children find it hard to speak about their experiences, but find drawing helpful to let out emotions they have bottled up.*

▲ *Children gingerly pick their way to school through a street lined with badly damaged buildings.*

SWAT VALLEY, PAKISTAN, 2005

I travelled to remote villages in the Swat Valley in Pakistan and on the Afghan border, where an organisation called Khwendo Kor was co-ordinating classes in homes and courtyards. In one school that I visited, the young teacher, whose only qualification was that she had completed primary school, had nothing more than a blackboard and a few books, but the pupils couldn't have been more enthusiastic. They sat in the hot sun concentrating on gaining knowledge. Girls realise that education is the only way for them to avoid a lifetime of isolation in the home, where the only people they meet would be their husband, children and female relatives.

These lessons were allowed only after long meetings with the community elders, but everyone was fearful and unsure of the future safety of their classes. One teacher had already been shot and left for dead. When a newspaper published the story and printed her name, some of her family disowned her, believing she had brought shame on them.

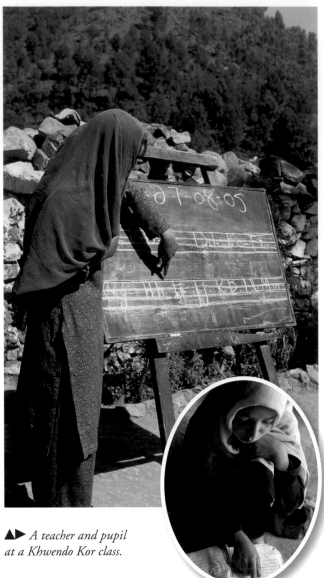

▲▶ *A teacher and pupil at a Khwendo Kor class.*

▼ *Supporters of Malala demonstrate outside the British Prime Minister's home in London, England, in October, 2012.*

In October 2012, 15-year-old Pakistani schoolgirl, Malala Yousafzai, was shot in the head and chest by the Taliban. She had campaigned for the right of girls to education. People all over the world were outraged and realised that, in many places, education is a right that has to be fought for. Malala became a worldwide icon for this cause and made people aware of the plight of girls in her country and elsewhere.

Malala was not the first, or only schoolgirl, to be attacked. Girls in Pakistan have had acid thrown at them at various times over the last 20 years, teachers have been killed and 96 schools were damaged or destroyed in 2012 – in 2011 the figure was even higher, at 152.

Of the 235 pupils at this school, 136 are girls.

▲ *Children head inside to begin their lessons at a primary school in Shomali Plain, 2006.*

AFGHANISTAN, 2006

Girls living in rural areas never had much access to education, but under the Taliban (1996–2001) all girls were forbidden to attend school. In spite of this, hundreds of pupils carried on studying in small groups at private homes. After the Taliban was ousted by NATO forces, girls' education was considered a priority and many new schools were built.

Unfortunately, not everyone agreed with such equality. Some schools were burned down, teachers were intimidated and there were even instances where school dinners and water were poisoned in girls' schools. Despite a climate of fear, girls' education is now flourishing and, besides studying, many are doing sports, including football, basketball and boxing.

▶ *Girls enjoy skipping at their new school.*

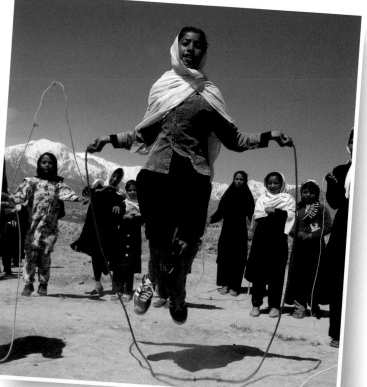

37

When a country is at war, schools soon close. Children may have a lot of time to play, but nothing to play with, or they are stuck at home because it's too dangerous to go out. However, some wars do lead to new opportunities for children. NGOs might set up activities, including pottery and art classes, for displaced children and refugees.

When families flee into exile, they are unlikely to include toys amongst the few possessions they take. Children often make their own toys from scrap materials they find lying around.

▼ *These boys from Sierra Leone scratch out their own games board on the ground.*

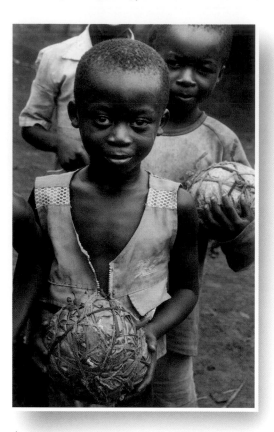

▲ *Young boys in CAR make their own footballs from scrap plastic tied tightly with crisscrossed string.*

▼ *All over Africa, boys enjoy hoop rolling, using whatever they can find for the hoop. This boy was playing in a refugee camp in Goma, the DRC, in 2008.*

◀ *This young girl was living on a landfill site in Kurdistan. She found this doll in the rubbish there.*

Qamar (shown collecting water on page 26) from Syria lamented how her life changed.

“ Before the war started we spent our time playing outside the house, but after it started we had to stay in all the time. We missed a lot of school – sometimes we only went once a week. Sometimes, we'd only be there an hour before we'd have to leave. A few times on our way home from school, there was shooting and we'd have to hide in a house. ”

Children in different parts of the world have different expectations. Teenage refugees from Syria used to computers and electronic games found it difficult when the limited power their family had came from solar lamps. But children are incredibly resourceful and are often able to make a game out of virtually nothing at all. In Jordan, I saw a little Syrian girl playing with a water bottle (above, right). She had dressed it in a red T-shirt and it was now her doll.

Hanifa attempts an "ollie" on her skateboard outside her house.

▲ *These Lebanese children have been sent Hula Hoops and skipping ropes by Save the Children.*

Charities that work with children have realised the importance of organising safe play areas within refugee camps, both to keep children busy and to stop them thinking too much about what they have lost. This may be as simple as finding teenagers who can organise games for younger children, or as complicated as building a whole playground. It all comes down to funding. If a charity can successfully raise enough money, it may supply Hula Hoops, swings and felt-tip pens to write and draw with.

AFGHANISTAN, 2011

There is now a thriving skateboard community in Kabul, thanks to the NGO Skateistan. Skateistan opened in 2009 and offers children free skateboarding lessons. It also provides opportunities for children to take part in classroom activities, and has around 350 students, just under half of which are girls. I met Hanifa, (shown left) the proud owner of a skateboard, who was keen to show me her skills. Living on a mountainside means that she has very little space to practise. She has a long walk to the park where she sells snacks, so she doesn't have much spare time.

▲ *Girls in Chad enthusiastically played volleyball, a donation from an aid organisation.*

THE PHOTOGRAPHER'S FINAL THOUGHTS

It is a privilege to be a photographer.

It can be exciting to be present when history is made, but it is also soul-destroying to earn a living from photographing misery and devastation. It's heartening when peace agreements are signed, warring factions forget their grievances and life can get back to relative normality. **"**

As a photographer I have to be careful with the photos I take. Pictures can be seen around the world once they are on the Internet, with no way to control who sees them. In some cultures, it is considered inappropriate for girls to be photographed. Even though a girl might be happy to have pictures taken, her wider family might not. In a volatile conflict, photos might be incriminating and used against the subject.

As photography has become cheaper and faster with the use of digital cameras and phones, people actually involved in a war have increasingly been able to photograph and film it themselves. With this goes the problem of verification, of distinguishing between news and propaganda, but photos – like words – are always subjective.

▼ If you had to choose one single photo to sum up Children Growing up with War, which of these three below would you choose?

CASE STUDY: STUDENTS' PHOTOGRAPHY PROJECT

Photography can be a powerful tool for change. This was vividly brought home to me when, after I facilitated a photography workshop for young people in Afghanistan, they produced an exhibition on the rights of the child.

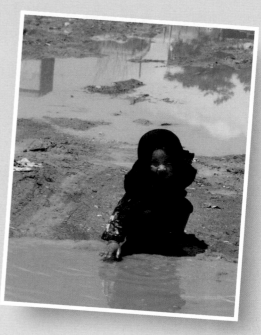

▲ The Right to Health, *by Mansoor*

"This is Mursal playing in a puddle. Sher is poor. She has no elder brother, but elder sisters."

▲ The Right to Education, *by Sesai*

▲ The Right to be Heard, *by Maryam*

"This photo shows that people are now free after a lot of war. Now we can learn and play and have fun."

▲ *One of my students photographs a shoeshine boy.*

43

MAP OF CONFLICTS

This map shows the countries referred to in this book. Not all of them are where conflicts are taking place.

GAZA
pages 13, 14, 35

UK
page 25

TUNISIA
pages 10 and 14

LIBYA
pages 10 and 14

CHAD
pages 3, 12, 41

SIERRA LEONE
pages 18, 22, 29, 32, 38

DARFUR
pages 12 and 34

THE DRC
pages 6, 7, 18, 21, 23, 26, 38

LEBANON
pages 8, 9, 25

SYRIA
pages 11, 20, 26, 39

AFGHANISTAN
pages 4, 15, 16, 17, 23, 24, 27, 28, 29, 30, 31, 32, 33, 37, 40, 41, 43

JORDAN
pages 11, 20, 26, 39

PAKISTAN
pages 33 and 36

VIETNAM
page 5

IRAQ
pages 3, 13, 24, 30, 34

SUDAN
pages 3, 12, 35

UGANDA
pages 3, 18, 35

RWANDA
pages 21 and 23

THE MAIN CONFLICTS

AFGHANISTAN

Afghanistan has been in conflict since the Soviet Union invaded it in 1979, to support its pro-communist regime. After the Soviets withdrew in 1989, civil war broke out between competing groups. In 1996, the Islamic fundamentalist Taliban took power, imposing strict Islamic law. This was especially harsh on women, who were not allowed to work, leave home or go to school. Following the 9/11 terrorist attacks on the United States, the US invaded Afghanistan and overthrew the Taliban. The country has, however, remained in conflict and civilians fled the violence. Today, more than 2.7 million Afghans live in exile – mainly in Pakistan and Iran. Afghanistan's living standards are among the lowest in the world. In many areas, there is a shortage of housing, clean water, electricity, medical care and jobs.

DARFUR

For decades, life in Darfur, western Sudan, has been precarious. Drought and food shortages have led to local conflicts over land and water. Civil war erupted in 2003, when rebels attacked government targets, accusing the government in Khartoum of neglecting black Africans in favour of Arabs. In response, the government-backed Arab Janjaweed militia attacked and razed Darfur's black African villages, killing many inhabitants. Hundreds of thousands fled to Chad, Uganda, Kenya and Ethiopia. The conflict continues. More than 1.4 million people (one fifth of the population) remain homeless, living in refugee camps. Hundreds of thousands of children have been born in camps and have known no other life.

DEMOCRATIC REPUBLIC OF THE CONGO (DRC)

In 1998, two armed rebel groups in the DRC, a huge central African country, attacked the Congolese army and started a deadly conflict for political power, and control of the country's rich mineral resources. Other African countries were drawn in. Angola, Namibia and Zimbabwe supported the army and Rwandan, Ugandan and Burundi troops supported the rebels. During the war, which lasted until 2003, an estimated 5.4 million people died – 90% of them due to disease and famine. Almost half of the deaths were of children under the age of 15. Two million people were internally displaced and hundreds of thousands, who fled the country, sought refuge in camps near the border. Today, there is renewed violence as armed rebel groups still clash. Civilians are still at risk from attack and continue to flee the country.

IRAQ

US, UK, Australian and Polish troops invaded Iraq in 2003 to depose Saddam Hussein, the Iraqi ruler, and prevent his use of suspected nuclear weapons (weapons of mass destruction), which the US and its allies claimed posed a threat to western security. The toppling of Saddam's government led to years of internal fighting, as conflicting groups competed for power. More than 4.5 million children lost one or both parents in the war. 70 per cent of schools were damaged or destroyed. Thousands of teachers and doctors fled overseas. Economic collapse led to increased poverty, malnutrition and more slums. Toxic heavy metals in modern weaponry are causing serious health problems and have led to birth defects. US troops left in 2011, but unrest, sectarian tension and violence continues.

LEBANON

In 2006, a 34-day conflict began between Hezbollah (a Shi'a Islamic militant group in Lebanon) and Israel. Hezbollah fighters captured two Israeli soldiers and killed several more in a cross-border raid. Outraged, Israel responded with bombs and missile strikes on towns, ports, power plants and the airport, leaving people without food, water or electricity. Tens of thousands of homes were destroyed or damaged. Hezbollah launched rockets into northern Israel and waged guerilla warfare with Israeli forces. More than a million Lebanese and up to half a million Israelis fled their homes. After the ceasefire, some parts of southern Lebanon were uninhabitable, because of unexploded Israeli cluster bomblets.

LIBYA

Colonel Gaddafi ruled oil-rich Libya for more than 40 years. In 2011, anti-government Libyans staged demonstrations, demanding change. Peaceful protest rapidly escalated into armed rebellion, as the government and rebel forces fought for control of major towns. Thousands of people fled to temporary shelter in Tunisia to escape the violence. After some months, the rebels stormed Libya's capital city Tripoli and, several weeks later, Gaddafi was captured and killed in his home town. A transitional government took charge, until elections for a General National Congress were held in 2012, the country's first free national election in six decades. There is still sporadic violence and thousands of people have not been able to return home.

RWANDA

There had long been animosity between the majority Hutus and minority Tutsis of Rwanda. In 1994, Hutus blamed Tutsis for the death of the Hutu president, whose plane was shot down. Over the next 100 days, unofficial Hutu militia, soldiers, policemen and ordinary civilians slaughtered hundreds of thousands of Tutsis with machetes, clubs and knives. The genocide ended when the Rwanda Patriotic Front (RPF), a military force of exiled Tutsis, took over the country. Fearing retribution, two million Hutus fled to the DRC. Thousands died of diseases, that spread quickly in overcrowded camps.

SIERRA LEONE

Civil war raged between 1991 and 2002 in this diamond-rich country. Rebels tried to overthrow successive governments, accusing them of corruption and mismanagement of the country's rich mineral resources. In a campaign of terror, the rebels murdered, looted, raped and mutilated innocent civilians. They abducted thousands of children for use as soldiers, labourers or 'wives'. The UN intervened in 1999, persuading both sides to sign a peace agreement. Peacekeeping forces disarmed the rebels. In 2009, three rebel leaders were sentenced to long jail terms for the civil war atrocities.

SYRIA

In 2011, protests against President Assad, whose family has ruled Syria for more than 40 years, were met with a lethal crackdown by government troops. The protests rapidly escalated into civil war across the country. More than 80,000 civilians have been killed. Almost 4 million Syrians have fled their homes, either to safer places in Syria, or across the border to Jordan, Turkey or Lebanon. Syria has been home to a large number of urban refugees from Iraq and elsewhere. These people have also had to flee, often back to unsafe futures in their own countries.

UGANDA

Initially founded as a militia claiming to defend the Acholi people in northern Uganda, the Lord's Resistance Army (LRA) has become a personality cult around its present leader, Joseph Kony. Known for its brutality, the LRA carried out vicious attacks in remote regions, murdering most of the adult population, mutilating the rest and abducting children. Boys became fighters. Girls became sex slaves. Eventually forced out of the country by the Ugandan army, the LRA has moved into the DRC, the Central African Republic and southern Sudan. It continues its savage raids.

WEBLINKS
TO ORGANISATIONS IN THIS BOOK

www.actionaid.org
Find out about ActionAid's projects, helping poor and marginalised people to eradicate poverty and overcome injustice and inequity in more than 45 countries.

www.baobabsurvivors.org
Read about how Baobab helps children and young people who have fled from political violence, torture and family loss in more than 20 war-torn countries.

www.care-international.org
Learn how CARE International provides civilians in war zones with places to go for food, shelter and support and helps the world's poorest people find routes out of poverty.

http://islamic-relief.com
Find out about the projects run across the world by Islamic Relief as they tackle the suffering of the world's poorest people.

www.khwendokor.org.pk
Discover the projects run by Khwendo Kor, which helps improve the health, education and skills of women and children in two poor, remote areas of Pakistan.

www.merlin.org.uk
Now part of Save the Children, learn about how Merlin sends doctors and nurses to global emergencies to save lives and care for the injured, as well as how it helps to improve the health of people who have suffered from war or famine.

www.msf.org
Find out what immediate and longer-term humanitarian medical aid Médecins Sans Frontières provides for victims of conflict and natural disasters.

www.photovoice.org
See how PhotoVoice works with NGOs around the world to give disadvantaged people the chance to represent themselves and create tools for positive social change.

www.savethechildren.net
Find out how Save the Children ensures that children affected by war get food, clean water and medical aid, as well as giving them safe places to learn and play.

www.skateistan.org
Be inspired by Skateistan, which uses skateboarding to engage hard-to-reach Afghan youth and provides them with education, skills and cross-cultural interaction.

www.unhcr.org
Research how the United Nations Refugee Agency co-ordinates action to safeguard the rights and well-being of refugees and resolve refugee problems worldwide.

GLOSSARY

baad a way of settling disputes between Afghan families, by giving away a girl to the family of the victim of a crime

bride price money, goods or property that a husband's family gives to his wife's family when they marry

cholera an acute bacterial infection, caused by drinking contaminated water, which can be fatal to young children

civil war a war between people within the same country

defoliant a chemical that makes plant leaves fall off

fixer a local person with good contacts

friendly fire when a military force is fired upon from one's own side

fundamentalist one who supports a religious movement that believes in interpreting its sacred text as truth

genocide the systematic, deliberate killing of a large number of a particular racial or cultural group

human rights the basic freedoms to which all humans are entitled, including life, liberty, thought, expression and equality

immunisation protective vaccination against diseases, such as polio, measles, mumps, rubella and diphtheria

internally displaced people (IDP) people forced to flee their homes, but who remains within their own country

land mine an explosive charge, hidden just under the ground, designed to blast enemy targets as they pass over it

malaria a fever, often fatal for children, caused by a parasite and spread by the bite of an infected mosquito

national service short-term compulsory participation in the armed services during peacetime

rebel someone who resists an established government with armed force

reconciliation the re-establishment of friendly relations between opposing groups after a conflict

refugees people forced to move to another country when they no longer feel safe in their own, because of war, religious persecution or natural disaster

Shi'a a branch of Islam followed by 20 per cent of the world's Muslims

Sunni the mainstream branch of Islam, followed by 80 per cent of the world's Muslims

Taliban an extreme Islamic group that seized power in Afghanistan and imposed a strict Muslim regime

INDEX